MAJOR BODIES OI

Arabian Sea
Baltic Sea
Bering Sea
Black Sea
Caribbean Sea
East China Sea
Gulf of Mexico
Mediterranean Sea
Red Sea
Sea of Japan
Sea of Okhotsk
South China Sea
Yellow Sea

merica)

AFRICA

Algeria

Capital: Algiers
Land Area: 918,497 square miles
Population: 22,817,000

Interesting Fact:

Algeria is a hot, dry country. Much of it is covered by the Sahara Desert, the world's largest desert.

Angola

Capital: Luanda
Land Area: 481,353 square miles
Population: 8,164,000

Interesting Fact:

Many native tribes live in the southern part of Angola, including the Xhosa, Hottentots and the Bushmen.

Benin

Capital: Porto-Novo
Land Area: 43,483 square miles
Population: 4,141,000

1

Interesting Fact:

Children living in villages along Benin's lagoons go to school in dugout canoes instead of school buses.

Botswana

Capital: Gaborone
Land Area: 231,804 square miles
Population: 1,104,000

Interesting Fact:

The Kalahari Desert, which covers most of Botswana, makes the country hot and dry.

Burkina Faso

Capital: Ouagadougou
Land Area: 105,869 square miles
Population: 7,084,000

Interesting Fact:

The name of this land-locked country means "land of the honest people."

Burundi

Capital: Bujumbura
Land Area: 10,759 square miles
Population: 4,807,000

Interesting Fact:

Natives known as the Watusi and Pygmy live in this country. Some Watusi grow to be seven feet tall, but Pygmies only average about four-and-one-half feet in height.

Cameroon

Capital: Yaounde
Land Area: 185,568 square miles
Population: 10,008,000

Interesting Fact:

Most of the Cameroon people are farmers.

Cape Verde

Capital: Praia
Land Area: 1,557 square miles
Population: 318,000

Interesting Fact:

Cape Verde consists of 15 mountainous islands. These islands are volcanic in origin and have little flat land.

Central African Republic

Capital: Bangui
Land Area: 240,534 square miles
Population: 2,744,000

Interesting Fact:

Many roads in the Central African Republic wash out during the rainy season.

Chad

Capital: N'Djamena
Land Area: 495,755 square miles
Population: 5,231,000

Interesting Fact:

Between the dry and rainy seasons, Lake Chad can vary from 3,800 to 9,900 square miles. Hippopotamuses, crocodiles and cranes live around the lake.

Comoros

Capital: Moroni
Land Area: 838 square miles
Population: 420,000

Interesting Fact:

Moslem sultans controlled the islands of Comoros until the French began taking them over in the mid-1800s.

Congo

Capital: Brazzaville

Land Area: 132,046 square miles
Population: 1,853,000

Interesting Fact:

Brazzaville, the capital city, is located on the Congo River. The sixth-longest river in the world, the Congo flows 2,900 miles and carries more water than any other river except the Amazon in South America.

Côte d'Ivoire

Capital: Abidjan
Land Area: 124,503 square miles
Population: 10,500,000

Interesting Fact:

This country became known as Ivory Coast after Europeans traded for ivory here. In 1985 the country's name was officially changed to Côte d'Ivoire.

Djibouti

Capital: Djibouti
Land Area: 8,494 square miles
Population: 304,000

Interesting Fact:

Because of its location on the Gulf of Aden, the capital of this small republic is an important seaport.

Egypt

Capital: Cairo
Land Area: 386,650 square miles
Population: 50,525,000

Interesting Facts:

Ancient Egyptians built many pyramids as tombs for the pharaohs. The Great Pyramids at Giza were one of the seven wonders of the ancient world and the only one substantially surviving today.

The Nile River flows north through Egypt. At 4,145 miles in length, many geographers consider it the longest river in the world.

The city of Amman has a camel racetrack, much like horse racetracks in other countries.

Equatorial Guinea

Capital: Malabo
Land Area: 10,832 square miles
Population: 359,000

Interesting Fact:

The first known white gorilla was found in Equatorial Guinea. It was named Snowflake.

Ethiopia

Capital: Addis Ababa
Land Area: 471,776 square miles
Population: 43,882,000

Interesting Fact:

A series of droughts that began in 1972 brought crop failures and serious food shortages. Hundreds of thousands of Ethiopians died from starvation. Worldwide relief efforts began in 1984 to help the millions of people still suffering here.

Gabon

Capital: Libreville
Land Area: 103,346 square miles
Population: 1,017,000

Interesting Fact:

Albert Schweitzer, the famous medical missionary, made his home in Gabon. He established a hospital and a leper colony near the town of Lambaréné.

The Gambia

Capital: Banjul
Land Area: 4,361 square miles
Population: 774,000

Interesting Fact:

Most farmers in Gambia raise peanuts.

Ghana

Capital: Accra

Land Area: 92,098 square miles
Population: 13,552,000

Interesting Fact:

Because the Portuguese found large deposits of gold here, Europeans once referred to this country as the "Gold Coast."

Guinea

Capital: Conakry
Land Area: 94,964 square miles
Population: 5,734,000

Interesting Fact:

Guinea has large natural deposits of bauxite, which is used to make aluminum.

Guinea-Bissau

Capital: Bissau
Land Area: 13,948 square miles
Population: 858,000

Interesting Fact:

Because Guinea-Bissau has very few paved roads, many residents must travel by boats along its rivers and Atlantic coastline.

Kenya

Capital: Nairobi
Land Area: 224,960 square miles
Population: 21,044,000

Interesting Facts:

Mount Kenya is the second-highest mountain in Africa. It rises to a height of 17,058 feet.

Many kinds of wildlife live in Kenya, including lions, zebras, elephants, giraffes and antelopes.

Lesotho

Capital: Maseru
Land Area: 11,716 square miles
Population: 1,552,000

Interesting Fact:

Lesotho is called the "Switzerland of Southern Africa" because its beautiful mountain scenery reminds people of the Swiss Alps.

Liberia

Capital: Monrovia
Land Area: 38,250 square miles
Population: 2,307,000

Interesting Fact:

Liberia was founded in 1821 as a refuge for freed American slaves.

Libya

Capital: Tripoli
Land Area: 679,359 square miles
Population: 3,876,000

Interesting Fact:

The Sahara Desert covers most of Libya.

Madagascar

Capital: Antananarivo
Land Area: 226,657 square miles
Population: 10,227,000

Interesting Fact:

Madagascar is situated on the fourth-largest island in the world. Many smaller islands are also part of this country.

Malawi

Capital: Lilongwe
Land Area: 45,747 square miles
Population: 7,292,000

Interesting Fact:

Women are the heads of the family in native Malawi tribes.

Mali

Capital: Bamako

Land Area: 478,764 square miles
Population: 7,898,000

Interesting Fact:

The legendary city of Timbuktu lies within this Moslem country. After a visit to Mecca in Saudi Arabia, King Mansa Musa built the Sankore Mosque here.

Mauritania

Capital: Nouakchott
Land Area: 397,954 square miles
Population: 1,691,000

Interesting Facts:

Almost all the workers in Mauritania are farmers or livestock herders.

Mauritania has relatively few educated people. Only about 20 students complete high school each year.

Mauritius

Capital: Port Louis
Land Area: 790 square miles
Population: 1,020,900

Interesting Fact:

This island nation has black volcanic peaks and vast sugar cane fields.

Morocco

Capital: Rabat
Land Area: 172,413 square miles
Population: 23,667,000

Interesting Fact:

Moroccan brides traditionally keep their eyes closed during their wedding ceremonies. An old custom says that if a bride looks up, an evil spirit may look into her eye and cause harm.

Mozambique

Capital: Maputo
Land Area: 309,494 square miles
Population: 14,022,000

Interesting Fact:

Mozambique allows some of its neighboring countries to use its excellent harbors along the Indian Ocean.

Namibia

Capital: Windhoek
Land Area: 320,827 square miles
Population: 1,203,000

Interesting Fact:

One of the largest game reserves in the world is in northern Namibia. Antelopes, cheetahs, giraffes, ostriches, lions, elephants and zebras roam there.

Niger

Capital: Niamey
Land Area: 489,189 square miles
Population: 6,715,000

Interesting Fact:

This country is named after the Niger River, which flows through its southwest corner. The third-longest river in Africa, it stretches 2,600 miles.

Nigeria

Capital: Lagos
Land Area: 356,667 square miles
Population: 105,448,000

Interesting Facts:

As they walk to market, Nigerian women balance their wares on their heads.

Children along Nigeria's western coast like to sit on leather mats and slide down rocks into the water below.

Rwanda

Capital: Kigali
Land Area: 10,169 square miles
Population: 6,489,000

Interesting Fact:

Many mountain gorillas live in Volcanoes National Park in northwestern Rwanda. The park is a refuge for this endangered species.

São Tomé and Principe

Capital: São Tomé
Land Area: 372 square miles
Population: 108,000

Interesting Fact:

Located just north of the equator, these two islands are 90 miles apart from each other and share a common government.

Senegal

Capital: Dakar
Land Area: 75,750 square miles
Population: 6,980,000

Interesting Fact:

Most Senegalian people live in rural areas. Most rural homes are mud huts with thatched roofs.

Seychelles

Capital: Victoria
Land Area: 171 square miles
Population: 67,000

Interesting Fact:

Seychelles consists of about 90 islands in the Indian Ocean.

Sierra Leone

Capital: Freetown
Land Area: 27,925 square miles
Population: 3,987,000

Interesting Fact:

Many diamonds come from Sierra Leone. It is the world's fifth-largest producer of industrial diamonds and sixth-largest producer of gem diamonds.

Somalia

Capital: Mogadishu
Land Area: 246,300 square miles
Population: 7,825,000

Interesting Fact:

Most Somalis are nomads who travel with their herds of camels, cattle, goats and sheep. They move frequently to find new grasslands for their herds.

South Africa

Capital: Bloemfontein (judicial)
       Cape Town (legislative)
       Pretoria (administrative)
Land Area: 423,359 square miles
Population: 33,241,000

Interesting Facts:

South Africa is the world's leading producer of both gold and gem diamonds.

Table Mountain stands behind the capital city of Cape Town. Many varieties of wildflowers grow on its flat top.

Sudan

Capital: Khartoum
Land Area: 966,757 square miles
Population: 22,932,000

Interesting Facts:

Sudan is the largest country in Africa.

The Nile River begins at a point where the Blue Nile and White Nile rivers meet. It flows northward through Egypt to the Mediterranean Sea.

Swaziland

Capital: Mbabane
Land Area: 6,704 square miles
Population: 692,000

Interesting Fact:

Even though Swazis rarely kill cattle for food, people with large herds of

cattle are highly respected. When a Swazi man marries, his family legal-
izes the marriage by giving cattle to his bride's family.

Tanzania

Capital: Dar-es-Salaam
Land Area: 364,886 square miles
Population: 22,415,000

Interesting Fact:

At 19,340 feet, Mount Kilimanjaro is Africa's highest mountain.

Togo

Capital: Lomé
Land Area: 21,622 square miles
Population: 3,118,000

Interesting Fact:

Most people in Togo are farmers. They grow enough food for their fami-
lies, but not enough to sell to others.

Tunisia

Capital: Tunis
Land Area: 63,170 square miles
Population: 7,424,000

Interesting Fact:

The ancient city of Carthage was in Tunisia. This powerful city rivaled
ancient Rome and played an important part in history.

Uganda

Capital: Kampala
Land Area: 93,354 square miles
Population: 15,158,000

Interesting Fact:

Lake Victoria, the largest lake in Africa, is the source of the White Nile
River.

Western Sahara

Capital: El Aaiun

Land Area: 102,700 square miles
Population: 150,000

Interesting Fact:

Morocco claims possession of this desert country, but Algeria and some residents of Western Sahara oppose it.

Zaire

Capital: Kinshasa
Land Area: 905,563 square miles
Population: 31,333,000

Interesting Fact:

Zaire has one of the world's largest and thickest rain forests. The forest covers about one-third of the country.

Zambia

Capital: Lusaka
Land Area: 290,586 square miles
Population: 7,054,000

Interesting Fact:

Lake Tanganyika, the second-largest lake in Africa, lies on the border between Zambia and Tanzania.

Zimbabwe

Capital: Harare
Land Area: 150,803 square miles
Population: 8,984,000

Interesting Fact:

Victoria Falls is on the border between Zimbabwe and Zambia. The falls drop 350 feet, sending up a spray that can be seen 10 miles away. In 1855 David Livingston became the first European to see the falls.

ANTARCTICA

Antarctica

Land Area: 5,400,000 square miles
Population: No permanent inhabitants

Interesting Facts:

Antarctica is covered almost entirely by an ice sheet and is not divided into countries like the other six continents.

Antarctica is cold all year long. Even in summer, temperatures remain below freezing in most parts of the continent.

In 1911 Norwegian explorer Roald Amundsen became the first man to reach the South Pole.

Penguins, flightless birds native to Antarctica, thrive on cold weather.

Blue whales, the largest animal in the world, also live here. Some blue whales are 100 feet long and weigh 150 tons. Of the many types of whales in Antarctica, killer whales are the most numerous.

ASIA

Afghanistan

Capital: Kabul
Land Area: 251,773 square miles
Population: 15,056,000

Interesting Fact:

The Khyber Pass is a narrow, 33-mile-long mountain pass between Pakistan and Afghanistan. Because Afghanistan is so mountainous, the pass is an important transportation route.

Bahrain

Capital: Manama
Land Area: 258 square miles
Population: 442,000

Interesting Fact:

After oil was discovered here in 1932, Bahrain became one of the richest countries along the Persian Gulf.

Bangladesh

Capital: Dhaka
Land Area: 55,598 square miles
Population: 104,204,000

Interesting Fact:

More than 266,000 people died when a cyclone and tidal wave struck Bangladesh in 1970.

Bhutan

Capital: Thimphu
Land Area: 18,147 square miles
Population: 1,446,000

Interesting Fact:

Bhutan is located high in the Himalayan Mountains.

Brunei

Capital: Bandar Seri Begawan
Land Area: 2,226 square miles
Population: 240,000

Interesting Fact:

Brunei became a wealthy country when oil was discovered offshore. However, the oil will probably run out early in the twenty-first century.

Burma

Capital: Rangoon
Land Area: 261,789 square miles
Population: 37,641,000

Interesting Fact:

Most people in Burma worship Buddha. The map shows the Buddhist temple in the capital city of Rangoon. There are many temples in this country.

China

Capital: Beijing
Land Area: 3,705,390 square miles
Population: 1,045,537,000

Interesting Facts:

China is the third-largest country in the world and the most populous.

The Forbidden City in Beijing was once a winter palace for the emperors. Ordinary citizens were forbidden to go near its gates.

The Great Wall of China was built more than 2,000 years ago to protect the Chinese from enemy attack. The wall is about 2,000 miles long and ranges from 15 to 50 feet in height. A road about 10 feet wide runs along its top.

Giant pandas live in China. Weighing from 165 to 350 pounds, adult pandas resemble large, roly-poly teddy bears. A panda's thick, wooly coat is mostly white, with black legs, ears and eye patches. A black band runs across its shoulders.

Sailing boats called junks are common along China's coastal waters.

The Chang Jiang River, also known as the Yangtze, is the longest river in China and one of the busiest waterways in the world. It runs for 3,964 miles. Another important river is the Hwang He, or Yellow River. This river was nicknamed China's Sorrow because of damage caused by flooding along its 2,903-mile course.

Cyprus

Capital: Nicosia
Land Area: 3,572 square miles
Population: 673,000

Interesting Fact:

The Cypriot economy relies heavily on tourism.

India

Capital: New Delhi
Land Area: 1,266,595 square miles
Population: 783,940,000

Interesting Facts:

India has the second-largest population in the world. Only China has more people.

The Taj Mahal, considered one of the world's most beautiful buildings, is located in Agra. An emperor built it about 300 years ago as a tomb for his favorite wife.

Most Indian people are Hindus. Because cows are holy in the Hindu religion, cattle roam freely in the streets and people are forbidden to harm them.

The Hindus believe the Ganges River is sacred. They believe that bathing in its waters washes away sin.

Indonesia

Capital: Jakarta
Land Area: 735,268 square miles
Population: 176,764,000

Interesting Fact:

Indonesia consists of several thousand islands, tiny islets and parts of larger islands.

Iran

Capital: Teheran
Land Area: 636,293 square miles
Population: 46,604,000

Interesting Fact:

Iran was once the center of the great Persian Empire. Many ruins can be seen throughout the country, including the remains of the empire's capital city, Persepolis.

Iraq

Capital: Baghdad
Land Area: 167,924 square miles
Population: 16,019,000

Interesting Fact:

Mesopotamia, one of the world's earliest civilizations, was based in what is now Iraq. The ancient ruins of the city of Babylon are an important tourist attraction. Mesopotamia means "land between the rivers." Babylon is located between the Tigris and Euphrates rivers.

Israel

Capital: Jerusalem
Land Area: 7,847 square miles
Population: 4,208,000

Interesting Facts:

The Dead Sea, a body of salt water about 50 miles long and 10 miles wide, lies between Israel and Jordan. The world's lowest body of water, it is

1,292 feet below sea level. No rivers flow out of the Dead Sea. Most of its waters are carried off through evaporation caused by Israel's hot climate. Because the sea is seven times saltier than the world's oceans, swimmers can't sink and fish can't live in its waters.

The Dead Sea Scrolls were found near the Dead Sea in 1947. They are the oldest surviving biblical documents.

Japan

Capital: Tokyo
Land Area: 145,856 square miles
Population: 121,402,000

Interesting Facts:

One of the greatest works of art in Japan is the 42-foot-tall bronze statue of Buddha at Kamakura. Its eyes are gold and a 30-pound lump of silver in its forehead represents Buddha's bump of wisdom. The statue was housed in a temple which was later destroyed by an earthquake.

Mount Fuji, an inactive volcano, is the highest peak in Japan. It rises 12,389 feet.

Jordan

Capital: Amman
Land Area: 37,737 square miles
Population: 2,756,000

Interesting Fact:

The ancient city of Jericho dates back to 8000 B.C. According to the Bible, Joshua took the city from the Canaanites and destroyed it. A modern town now sits near the site.

Kampuchea

Capital: Phnom Penh
Land Area: 69,898 square miles
Population: 6,388,000

Interesting Facts:

Officially called Democratic Kampuchea, this country is also known as Cambodia.

The Mekong River flows south from Laos through Kampuchea and Vietnam, then empties into the South China Sea.

18

Kuwait

Capital: Kuwait
Land Area: 6,880 square miles
Population: 1,771,000

Interesting Fact:

Kuwait is one of the world's leading oil producers.

Laos

Capital: Vientiane
Land Area: 91,428 square miles
Population: 3,679,000

Interesting Fact:

Farmers in Laos use oxen to pull wooden plows.

Lebanon

Capital: Beirut
Land Area: 4,015 square miles
Population: 2,674,000

Interesting Fact:

The early Phoenicians lived in Lebanon as early as 3000 B.C. Our modern alphabet evolved from the one used by the Phoenicians.

Malaysia

Capital: Kuala Lumpur
Land Area: 127,316 square miles
Population: 15,820,000

Interesting Fact:

Monkeys help Malaysian farmers harvest coconuts.

Maldives

Capital: Male
Land Area: 115 square miles
Population: 179,000

Interesting Fact:

This country consists of about 2,000 small coral islands.

Mongolia

Capital: Ulan Bator
Land Area: 604,247 square miles
Population: 1,942,000

Interesting Fact:

The Gobi Desert covers most of Mongolia.

Nepal

Capital: Kathmandu
Land Area: 56,136 square miles
Population: 17,422,000

Interesting Fact:

Mount Everest, the tallest mountain in the world, is in Nepal. Its peak rises 29,000 feet--more than five miles up. In 1953 Sir Edmund Hillary and Tenzing Norgay became the first climbers to reach the top.

North Korea

Capital: Pyongyang
Land Area: 46,540 square miles
Population: 20,543,000

Interesting Facts:

The Korean War, one of the bloodiest wars in history, began when Communist-ruled North Korea invaded South Korea in 1950. Until a 1953 truce ended the hostilities, about four million soldiers and civilians were killed, wounded or reported missing.

Because North Korea has a good supply of mineral deposits and inexpensive hydroelectric power, the country's economy is helped by manufacturing.

Oman

Capital: Muscat
Land Area: 82,030 square miles
Population: 1,271,000

Interesting Fact:

The Strait of Hormuz is at the northern tip of Oman. Much of the world's oil is shipped through this waterway.

Pakistan

Capital: Islamabad
Land Area: 310,403 square miles
Population: 101,855,000

Interesting Fact:

The Indus River is about 1,800 miles long and flows through Pakistan. Early civilizations began along this river more than 4,500 years ago.

Philippines

Capital: Manila
Land Area: 115,831 square miles
Population: 58,091,000

Interesting Fact:

Early Filipinos used bolo knives to carve out high terraces on the mountainsides. Farmers have grown rice on these flooded terraces ever since they were built.

Qatar

Capital: Doha
Land Area: 4,247 square miles
Population: 305,000

Interesting Fact:

Oil is Qatar's most important product.

Saudi Arabia

Capital: Riyadh
Land Area: 839,996 square miles
Population: 11,519,000

Interesting Facts:

Saudi Arabia exports more oil than any other country.

The Rub' al Khali Desert in southern Saudi Arabia is practically unexplored. The name of this desert translates into "empty quarter."

Striped water towers exist in some parts of the Arabian deserts.

Mecca is the sacred city of the followers of Islam and the birthplace of their prophet, Mohammed. People of other faiths are forbidden to enter the city.

Singapore

Capital: Singapore
Land Area: 224 square miles
Population: 2,584,000

Interesting Fact:

Every year thousands of ships dock at Singapore, an important seaport.

South Korea

Capital: Seoul
Land Area: 38,025 square miles
Population: 43,284,000

Interesting Facts:

Between 500,000 and one million South Korean civilians died during the Korean War between 1950 and 1953.

Scientists have found stone artifacts showing that people lived here 30,000 years ago.

Sri Lanka

Capital: Colombo
Land Area: 25,332 square miles
Population: 16,638,000

Interesting Fact:

Sri Lanka means "beautiful island."

Syria

Capital: Damascus
Land Area: 71,498 square miles
Population: 10,931,000

Interesting Fact:

One of the world's oldest cities, Damascus is thought to be 5,000 years old.

Taiwan

Capital: Taipei
Land Area: 13,885 square miles
Population: 19,601,000

Interesting Fact:

When the Communists took over mainland China in 1949, the Chinese Nationalist government reestablished itself on this island. For many years the country was known as Formosa.

Thailand

Capital: Bangkok
Land Area: 198,456 square miles
Population: 52,438,000

Interesting Facts:

Siamese cats received their name from this Far Eastern country, which was once called Siam.

Elephants do heavy work in Thailand. They help move logs in rain forests where there are no roads for trucks.

Turkey

Capital: Ankara
Land Area: 301,381 square miles
Population: 51,819,000

Interesting Facts:

Turkey's largest city, Istanbul, is located on two continents. Its European and Asian sections are divided by the Bosporus, a strait that connects the Black Sea with the Sea of Marmara.

Mount Ararat, where Noah's Ark is said to have landed after the flood, is in Turkey.

Many Moslems worship in the 1,400-year-old Mosque of St. Sophia. Its walls are covered with pictures made from bits of colored glass set in gold backgrounds. Light enters the mosque from 40 windows set in its dome.

Union of Soviet Socialist Republics

Information on this country is listed under the section on Europe.

United Arab Emirates

Capital: Abu Dhabi
Land Area: 32,000 square miles
Population: 1,326,000

Interesting Fact:

Seven Arab states combined to form the United Arab Emirates in 1971.

Vietnam

Capital: Hanoi
Land Area: 128,401 square miles
Population: 61,994,000

Interesting Facts:

North Vietnam's desire to unify North and South Vietnam under Communist rule led to a destructive war that lasted about eighteen years. Between 1965 and 1973, more than 57,000 American soldiers died trying to protect South Vietnam, which eventually fell to the Communist forces in 1975.

Agriculture is Vietnam's principal industry. Rice is its biggest crop.

Yemen, People's Democratic Republic

Capital: Aden
Land Area: 128,559 square miles
Population: 2,275,000

Interesting Fact:

Most of Yemen's land is hot and dry. Only a few areas can be farmed successfully.

Yemen Arab Republic

Capital: Sanaa
Land Area: 75,290 square miles
Population: 6,339,000

Interesting Fact:

This country is famous for its mocha coffee.

AUSTRALIA AND OCEANIA

Australia

Capital: Canberra
Land Area: 2,966,200 square miles
Population: 15,763,000

Interesting Facts:

Australia is one of the world's leading producers of wool. Sheep are raised on Australian ranches called sheep stations.

Aborigines are Australia's native people. They were the first people to use a boomerang, an unusual, curve-shaped weapon made from hardwood. When a boomerang is thrown properly, it returns to the person who threw it.

Sydney is Australia's largest city. It has many modern buildings, such as the Opera House pictured on the map.

Australia is the home of many unusual animals. Among them are the kangaroo, platypus, wallaby, wombat, dingo, emu and koala.

Fiji

Capital: Suva
Land Area: 7,056 square miles
Population: 715,000

Interesting Fact:

Many Fijians do not have furniture in their homes. When they go to bed, they unroll a mat and sleep on the floor.

Kiribati

Capital: Tarawa
Land Area: 281 square miles
Population: 63,000

Interesting Fact:

Kiribati's 33 islands are spread out over two million square miles of the Pacific Ocean.

Nauru

Capital: The Yaren Administrative Centre
Land Area: 8 square miles
Population: 8,000

Interesting Fact:

This tiny, oval-shaped island is the third-smallest country in the world. Because it has no cities, its people all live in rural areas.

New Zealand

Capital: Wellington
Land Area: 103,736 square miles
Population: 3,305,000

Interesting Fact:

In the 1600s the first European settlers in this country met tall, light-skinned New Zealand natives called Maoris. Maoris still live in New Zealand villages today. They tattoo their faces with beautiful designs. When an important man dies, his head is dried and shrunken to preserve the patterns.

Papua New Guinea

Capital: Port Moresby
Land Area: 176,280 square miles
Population: 3,395,000

Interesting Fact:

Natives of Papua New Guinea often use outrigger canoes. An outrigger has a log fastened to its side to keep it from tipping over in rough water.

Solomon Islands

Capital: Honiara
Land Area: 10,640 square miles
Population: 283,000

Interesting Fact:

The largest of the Solomon islands is Guadalcanal. It was the site of some of the fiercest battles between the United States and Japan during World War II.

Tonga

Capital: Nuku'alofa
Land Area: 270 square miles
Population: 104,000

Interesting Facts:

Tonga consists of about 170 volcanic and coral islands. Only 25% of them are permanently inhabited.

No Tongan male over six can appear in public without wearing a shirt.

Tuvalu

Capital: Funafuti
Land Area: 10 square miles
Population: 8,580

Interesting Fact:

Because Tuvalu has poor soil, collecting and storing drinking water is difficult. Sometimes natives drink coconut milk instead of water.

Vanuatu

Capital: Vila
Land Area: 5,700 square miles
Population: 136,000

Interesting Fact:

Vanuatu's national anthem is "Yumi, Yumi, Yumi." "Yumi" means "we."

Western Samoa

Capital: Apia
Land Area: 1,133 square miles
Population: 165,000

Interesting Fact:

Robert Louis Stevenson, the author of *Treasure Island,* spent his final years in Western Samoa.

EUROPE

Albania

Capital: Tirana
Land Area: 11,100 square miles
Population: 3,020,000

Interesting Fact:

Albania is one of the poorest countries in Europe. Public worship and religious institutions are outlawed in this country, but many citizens still follow the Moslem, Roman Catholic and Greek Orthodox faiths.

Andorra

Capital: Andorra la Vella

Land Area: 185 square miles
Population: 49,000

Interesting Fact:

You can mail a letter for free in this small country. Andorra's postal system receives its operating funds by selling stamps to collectors around the world.

Austria

Capital: Vienna
Land Area: 32,374 square miles
Population: 7,546,000

Interesting Fact:

Mozart was born in Austria. A gifted and famous composer, he played music before he was old enough to go to school.

Belgium

Capital: Brussels
Land Area: 11,779 square miles
Population: 9,868,000

Interesting Fact:

The saxophone was invented by Adolphe Sax, a Belgian instrument maker.

Bulgaria

Capital: Sofia
Land Area: 44,365 square miles
Population: 8,990,000

Interesting Fact:

The Danube River forms the northern boundary of Bulgaria. The second-longest river in Europe, it flows 1,776 miles from Germany to the Black Sea.

Czechoslovakia

Capital: Prague
Land Area: 49,365 square miles
Population: 15,542,000

Interesting Fact:

Each winter visitors travel to Czechoslovakia to ski its mountain slopes.

Denmark

Capital: Copenhagen
Land Area: 16,633 square miles
Population: 5,097,000

Interesting Facts:

Hans Christian Andersen, author of "The Ugly Duckling" and other well-known fairy tales, was born in Denmark.

Greenland, the largest island in the world, belongs to Denmark. More than half the island lies under a huge ice cap. Glaciers flow down from Greenland's mountains and discharge a billion tons of ice into the sea each year.

East Germany

Capital: East Berlin
Land Area: 41,768 square miles
Population: 16,692,000

Interesting Fact:

Berlin became a divided city after Germany's defeat in World War II. In 1961 East Germany's Communist government erected a wall to keep East Berlin residents from fleeing to the Western sector.

Finland

Capital: Helsinki
Land Area: 130,119 square miles
Population: 4,931,000

Interesting Facts:

Lapps are the native people of northern Finland. Many Lapps traditionally have relied on herding and breeding reindeer for their livelihoods.

The sauna, a type of steam bath, was invented in Finland.

France

Capital: Paris
Land Area: 220,668 square miles
Population: 55,239,000

Interesting Fact:

Paris was founded on an island in the Seine River. The city's tallest structure, the Eiffel Tower, rises 984 feet high.

Greece

Capital: Athens
Land Area: 51,146 square miles
Population: 9,954,000

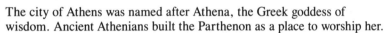

Interesting Facts:

The city of Athens was named after Athena, the Greek goddess of wisdom. Ancient Athenians built the Parthenon as a place to worship her.

Greece is considered the birthplace of modern civilization. More than 2,000 years ago the Greeks developed many of the concepts behind today's arts, sciences, law and democracy.

Hungary

Capital: Budapest
Land Area: 35,919 square miles
Population: 10,624,000

Interesting Fact:

With its seasonable climate and fertile soil, Hungary is ideally suited for agriculture. Most of its agricultural products are raised in large collective and state-owned farms.

Iceland

Capital: Reykjavík
Land Area: 39,769 square miles
Population: 244,000

Interesting Facts:

Iceland's volcanic rocks heat many hot springs and geysers. These warm waters are piped to buildings and hothouses for growing fruits, vegetables and flowers all year long. Farmers in some areas pipe this water through the soil to warm it for growing crops.

October 9 is Leif Ericsson Day. Ericsson was a Viking explorer who discovered North America around 1000 A.D.

Ireland

Capital: Dublin
Land Area: 27,137 square miles
Population: 3,624,000

Interesting Fact:

Dublin is famous for its fine linen cloth.

Italy

Capital: Rome
Land Area: 116,303 square miles
Population: 57,226,000

Interesting Facts:

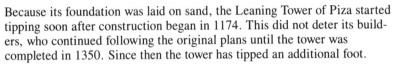

Because its foundation was laid on sand, the Leaning Tower of Piza started tipping soon after construction began in 1174. This did not deter its builders, who continued following the original plans until the tower was completed in 1350. Since then the tower has tipped an additional foot.

The city of Venice, one of Italy's most popular tourist attractions, sits on about 120 islands in the Adriatic Sea. It has canals instead of streets and people travel through the city on boats.

Liechtenstein

Capital: Vaduz
Land Area: 62 square miles
Population: 28,000

Interesting Fact:

One of the world's smallest countries, Liechtenstein has not fought in any war since 1866. The government abolished its army in 1868.

Luxembourg

Capital: Luxembourg
Land Area: 998 square miles
Population: 367,000

Interesting Fact:

The month-long Battle of the Bulge was partially fought in Luxembourg. The German army's failure to push back the invading Allied forces helped contribute to Germany's defeat in World War II.

Malta

Capital: Valletta
Land Area: 122 square miles
Population: 354,000

Interesting Fact:

A small breed of dog known as the Maltese originated in this island country about 2,500 years ago. Some experts consider this white, long-haired breed to be the world's first lap dog.

Monaco

Capital: Monaco-Ville
Land Area: 0.6 square miles
Population: 28,000

Interesting Fact:

According to a 1918 treaty, Monaco will come under French rule if Monaco's royal family has no male heirs.

Netherlands

Capital: Amsterdam
Land Area: 15,770 square miles
Population: 14,536,000

Interesting Fact:

The Netherlands is famous for tulips and windmills.

Norway

Capital: Oslo
Land Area: 125,181 square miles
Population: 4,165,000

Interesting Fact:

The adventuresome Vikings were based in Norway between the eighth and tenth centuries. Residents along Europe's coastlines feared the Vikings, who often raided and plundered their towns and villages.

Poland

Capital: Warsaw
Land Area: 120,727 square miles
Population: 37,546,000

Interesting Fact:

Pope John Paul II is a native of Poland. When elected to the papacy in 1978, he became the first non-Italian to head the Roman Catholic Church since 1523.

Portugal

Capital: Lisbon
Land Area: 35,553 square miles
Population: 10, 095,000

Interesting Fact:

Bullfighting is one of Portugal's most popular sports.

Romania

Capital: Bucharest
Land Area: 91,699 square miles
Population: 22,830,000

Interesting Fact:

People have traveled to Romania's springs since ancient times. Many believe that bathing in these waters is healthful.

San Marino

Capital: San Marino
Land Area: 24 square miles
Population: 23,000

Interesting Fact:

Located on the slopes of Mount Titano, San Marino is completely surrounded by Italy.

Spain

Capital: Madrid
Land Area: 194,896 square miles
Population: 39,074,000

Interesting Facts:

Spain is a major world producer of cork, which is taken from the outer bark of cork oak trees near the Mediterranean Sea.

The Rock of Gibraltar is south of Spain. This huge limestone rock is more than two miles long and 1,408 feet high.

Sweden

Capital: Stockholm
Land Area: 173,731 square miles
Population: 8,357,000

Interesting Fact:

Cross-country skiing is a popular Swedish sport.

Switzerland

Capital: Bern
Land Area: 15,941 square miles
Population: 6,466,000

Interesting Fact:

Switzerland is famous for its superior watchmakers and the breathtaking scenery of the Alps Mountains.

Turkey

Information on this country is listed under the section on Asia.

Union of Soviet Socialist Republics

Capital: Moscow
Land Area: 8,649,496 square miles
Population: 279,904,000

Interesting Facts:

The Soviet Union is the largest country in the world and has the third-largest population.

Two of Moscow's most famous sites are St. Basil's Cathedral and the Kremlin. St. Basil's Cathedral, recognized by its onion-shaped domes, was built in the sixteenth century during the reign of Ivan the Terrible. Many Russian buildings were modeled after it. The Kremlin, located on one side of the Red Square, was once the home of the czars. It is now the center of the Soviet Union's Communist government.

The Volga River, the longest river in Europe, flows through the Soviet Union. Two other large Soviet rivers, the Ob and the Lena, flow northward into the Arctic Ocean.

The Soviet Union contains several large lakes. One of them, the Caspian Sea, is considered the largest lake in the world. Another, Lake Baikal, is believed to be the world's deepest freshwater lake. Its maximum known depth is 5,715 feet.

Siberia stretches across northern Asia from the Ural Mountains to the Pacific Ocean. Part of this sparsely-populated region lies within the Arctic Circle, where winter temperatures can fall as low as 90 degrees below zero.

The Trans-Siberian Railroad links Moscow to Russia's Pacific coastline. The railroad, which took 25 years to build, was completed in 1916.

A 1988 earthquake devastated the Soviet republic of Armenia. An estimated 55,000 people died and 500,000 were left homeless.

United Kingdom

Capital: London, England
Land Area: 94,226 square miles
Population: 56,458,000

Interesting Facts:

The United Kingdom is made up of England, Scotland, Northern Ireland, Wales, and the islands of Guernsey, Jersey and the Isle of Man. It is also known as Great Britain.

Stonehenge, located in Wiltshire, England, is a mysterious group of large cut stones arranged in a circle. Some of these stones weigh as much as 26 tons. Experts believe Stonehenge was a site for sun-worshipping activities.

Vatican City

Land Area: 0.2 square mile
Population: 1,000

Interesting Facts:

Vatican City is the headquarters of the Roman Catholic Church and the home of its Pope.

The smallest independent country in the world, Vatican City is located within the city limits of Rome.

West Germany

Capital: Bonn

Land Area: 95,975 square miles
Population: 60,734,000

Interesting Fact:

When Germany was defeated in World War II, the United States, France and Britain disagreed with the Soviet Union as to how the country would be unified. In 1949 it was divided into two countries. The territory occupied by Western forces became West Germany; the land controlled by the Soviets became East Germany.

Yugoslavia

Capital: Belgrade
Land Area: 98,766 square miles
Population: 23,284,000

Interesting Fact:

Yugoslavia means "Land of the Southern Slavs." It got this name because most of its residents are Slavic.

NORTH AMERICA

Antigua and Barbuda

Capital: St. John's
Land Area: 171 square miles
Population: 82,000

Interesting Fact:

This country consists of three islands. One of them, Redonda, is an uninhabited rock that rises about 1,000 feet high.

The Bahamas

Capital: Nassau
Land Area: 5,380 square miles
Population: 235,000

Interesting Fact:

Christopher Columbus first landed in the New World at San Salvador in The Bahamas.

Barbados

Capital: Bridgetown

Land Area: 166 square miles
Population: 253,000

Interesting Fact:

Barbados is one of the most densely populated countries in the world. It averages more than 1,600 inhabitants per square mile.

Belize

Capital: Belmopan
Land Area: 8,867 square miles
Population: 168,400

Interesting Fact:

Belize was the United Kingdom's last colony on the American mainland. It achieved independence in 1981.

Canada

Capital: Ottawa
Land Area: 3,851,790 square miles
Population: 25,625,000

Interesting Facts:

An old fortress stands atop Cape Diamond in the city of Quebec. The original earthwork was built by the French in 1703. The English rebuilt the fortress from 1823 to 1832. Cannons remain in it to this day.

In 1873 the Canadian government established the Royal Canadian Mounted Police. Today there are 16,000 Mounties. "A Mountie always gets his man" is a popular old saying.

Horseshoe Falls is about a half-mile wide and drops about 160 feet. The falls lie between Lake Ontario and Lake Erie.

The Northwest Territories contain Canada's longest river, the Mackenzie, and its two largest lakes, Great Bear Lake and Great Slave Lake.

Costa Rica

Capital: San José
Land Area: 19,575 square miles
Population: 2,714,000

Interesting Fact:

The Spanish word "costa rica" means rich coast.

Cuba

Capital: Havana
Land Area: 44,218 square miles
Population: 10,221,000

Interesting Fact:

Soon after Fidel Castro gained control of the government in 1959, Cuba became the first Communist nation in the Western Hemisphere.

Dominica

Capital: Roseau
Land Area: 290 square miles
Population: 74,000

Interesting Fact:

Dominica is a mountainous island covered with dense tropical forests. Plant life thrives on its rich volcanic soil.

Dominican Republic

Capital: Santo Domingo
Land Area: 18,816 square miles
Population: 6,785,000

Interesting Fact:

Santo Domingo was the first city founded by Europeans in the Western Hemisphere.

El Salvador

Capital: San Salvador
Land Area: 8,260 square miles
Population: 5,105,000

Interesting Fact:

El Salvador is the smallest mainland country in the Western Hemisphere.

Grenada

Capital: St. George's
Land Area: 133 square miles
Population: 86,000

Interesting Fact:

Grenada is a major world producer of nutmeg, cocoa and bananas.

Guatemala

Capital: Guatemala City
Land Area: 42,042 square miles
Population: 8,600,000

Interesting Fact:

The marimba is a popular Guatemalan musical instrument. It has rows of hard wooden bars and is played with hammers.

Haiti

Capital: Port-au-Prince
Land Area: 10,714 square miles
Population: 5,870,000

Interesting Fact:

Haiti, which became an independent nation in 1804, is the oldest republic established by black people.

Honduras

Capital: Tegucigalpa
Land Area: 43,277 square miles
Population: 4,648,000

Interesting Fact:

Bananas are the leading crop in Honduras.

Jamaica

Capital: Kingston
Land Area: 4,232 square miles
Population: 2,288,000

Interesting Fact:

Jamaica is known for its unique music. Steel drum bands and reggae music are popular in this country.

Mexico

Capital: Mexico City

Land Area: 761,604 square miles
Population: 81,709,000

Interesting Facts:

Mexico was the center of the Aztec and Mayan Indian civilizations. Visitors can still see the ruins of their great cities, as well as large pyramids honoring the sun and moon.

Bullfighting remains a popular Mexican spectator sport.

Nicaragua

Capital: Managua
Land Area: 50,193 square miles
Population: 3,342,000

Interesting Fact:

Nicaragua is the largest country in Central America.

Panama

Capital: Panama City
Land Area: 29,208 square miles
Population: 2,227,000

Interesting Fact:

The Panama Canal connects the Atlantic and Pacific oceans. It is considered one of the great engineering feats of the twentieth century.

St. Christopher and Nevis

Capital: Basseterre
Land Area: 101 square miles
Population: 40,000

Interesting Fact:

The economy of St. Christopher and Nevis is based on sugar cane production and tourism.

St. Lucia

Capital: Castries
Land Area: 238 square miles
Population: 123,000

Interesting Fact:

Almost all residents of St. Lucia are descendants of African slaves.

St. Vincent and the Grenadines

Capital: Kingstown
Land Area: 150 square miles
Population: 103,000

Interesting Fact:

This tiny Caribbean island nation is a major exporter of bananas.

Trinidad and Tobago

Capital: Port-of-Spain
Land Area: 1,980 square miles
Population: 1,204,000

Interesting Fact:

Trinidad is famous for calypso music and the limbo dance.

United States

Capital: Washington, D.C.
Land Area: 3,623,420 square miles
Population: 240,856,000

Interesting Facts:

The White House is in Washington, D.C., the capital of the United States. It has been the home of American presidents since 1800.

The Statue of Liberty in New York Harbor was a gift from France to the United States. It is a welcoming sign of freedom to all people who come to America.

The Mississippi River is the longest river in the United States, flowing south into the Gulf of Mexico.

The Grand Canyon is one of the seven natural wonders of the world. Its deep gorge was formed over a period of 10 million years.

Mount Rushmore is in the Black Hills of South Dakota. The faces of United States presidents George Washington, Thomas Jefferson, Theodore Roosevelt and Abraham Lincoln are carved on the side of this mountain.

The Golden Gate Bridge in San Francisco, California, is one of the world's longest suspension bridges. It stretches 4,200 feet between two high towers.

Alaska's native people, the Inuits, are also known as Eskimos. During the long Arctic winters many Inuits traveled using sleds pulled by dog teams. Today snowmobiles are replacing dog teams.

Hawaii is the only state entirely surrounded by ocean. Many of its volcanoes are still active. Hawaii is a major world producer of pineapples.

SOUTH AMERICA

Argentina

Capital: Buenos Aires
Land Area: 1,065,189 square miles
Population: 31,186,000

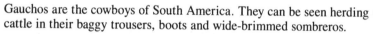

Interesting Facts:

Gauchos are the cowboys of South America. They can be seen herding cattle in their baggy trousers, boots and wide-brimmed sombreros.

A statue known as "Christ of the Andes" was erected in the Andes Mountains after a war between Argentina and Chile was settled. It was made from the melted cannons of both countries. An inscription on the statue says the mountains will crumble into dust before the countries break their promises to keep peace.

Bolivia

Capital: La Paz (legal)
           Sucre (de facto)
Land Area: 424,165 square miles
Population: 6,200,000 square miles

Interesting Fact:

Lake Titicaca is on the boundary between Peru and Bolivia. At 12,500 feet above sea level, it is one of the highest lakes in the world.

Brazil

Capital: Brasília
Land Area: 3,286,470 square miles
Population: 143,277,000

Interesting Facts:

To encourage people to move away from its crowded Eastern coastline, the Brazilian government built a new capital city about 600 miles inland. The city, Brasília, was completed in 1960.

The Amazon is one of the world's longest rivers. Estimates of its length vary from 4,000 to 4,195 miles. More water flows through the Amazon than any other river in the world. Alligators live along its banks, and piranha fish and electric eels can be found in its waters.

Chile

Capital: Santiago
Land Area: 292,257 square miles
Population: 12,261,000

Interesting Facts:

Chile's Atacama Desert is one of the world's driest places.

Chile owns Easter Island in the Pacific Ocean. Statues of male heads and shoulders stand on these islands. Some are 36 feet tall and weigh as much as 50 tons. The statues are estimated to be between 400 and 1,000 years old. No one knows who carved them or how they were lifted onto their stone platforms.

Colombia

Capital: Bogotá
Land Area: 439,735 square miles
Population: 29,956,000

Interesting Fact:

Colombia was named after Christopher Columbus.

Ecuador

Capital: Quito
Land Area: 109,483 square miles
Population: 9,647,000

Interesting Fact:

Ecuador is the Spanish word for "equator," the imaginary line that divides the earth's Northern and Southern hemispheres.

French Guiana

Capital: Cayenne
Land Area: 32,252 square miles
Population: 85,700

Interesting Fact:

Devil's Island, located off the coast of French Guiana, was used by France as a prison colony for more than 100 years. The last prisoners left the island after World War II.

Guyana

Capital: Georgetown
Land Area: 83,000 square miles
Population: 771,000

Interesting Fact:

Guyana is the only English-speaking country in South America.

Paraguay

Capital: Asunción
Land Area: 157,047 square miles
Population: 4,119,000

Interesting Fact:

Paraguay has the only national flag with a different design on each side.

Peru

Capital: Lima
Land Area: 496,222 square miles
Population: 20,207,000

Interesting Fact:

The city of Cuzco was the capital of the ancient Incan empire. This civilization once covered most of Peru, Bolivia and Ecuador, and parts of Colombia, Chile and Argentina.

Suriname

Capital: Paramaribo
Land Area: 63,037 square miles
Population: 381,000